Published by Ali Gator Productions.

First Published 2017

National Library of Australia Cataloguing-in-Publication (CIP) data:
Ahmad Zakky, Say Alhamdulillah
ISBN 978-1-921772-42-9
For primary school age, Juvenile fiction, Dewey Number: 823.92

ALI GATOR

T: +61 (3) 9386 2771 F: +61 (3) 9478 8854
P.O. Box 2536, Regent West, Melbourne Victoria, 3072 Australia
E: info@ali-gator.com W: www.ali-gator.com

Abdul was so happy.
He just received a gift,
a brand new toy car.

"Ha ha Yasmeen, I've got a new toy,"
said Abdul cheekily.

"I've got one too, **Alhamdulillah**,"
said Yasmeen while showing
a cute doll to Abdul.

ALHAMDULILLAH - PRAISE BE TO ALLAH

"Abdul, you have to say **Alhamdulillah**," stated Yasmeen.

"What for?" asked Abdul.

"If Allah gives you anything, we should be grateful by saying **Alhamdulillah**," Yasmeen explained, trying to stay calm.

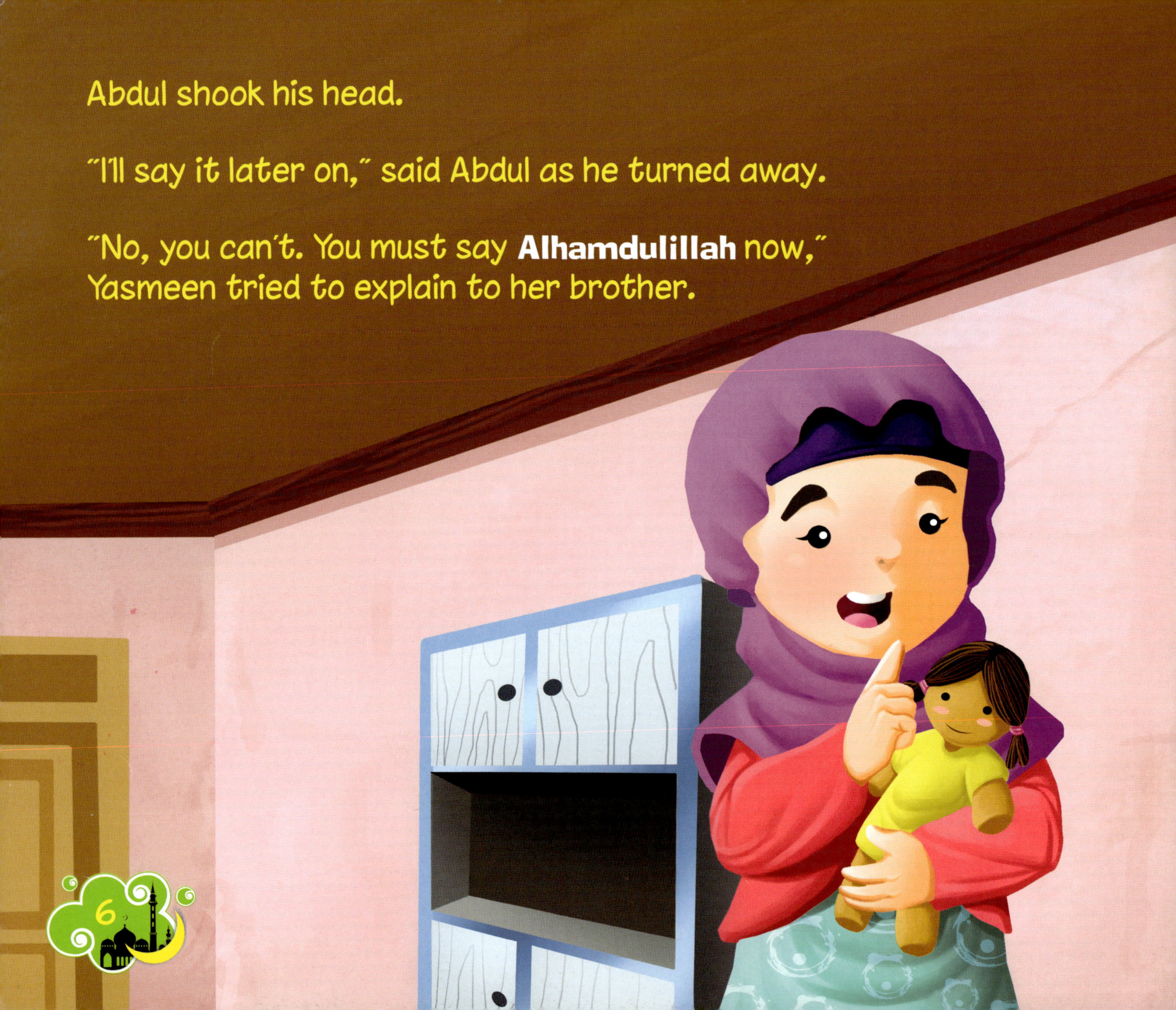

Abdul shook his head.

"I'll say it later on," said Abdul as he turned away.

"No, you can't. You must say **Alhamdulillah** now," Yasmeen tried to explain to her brother.

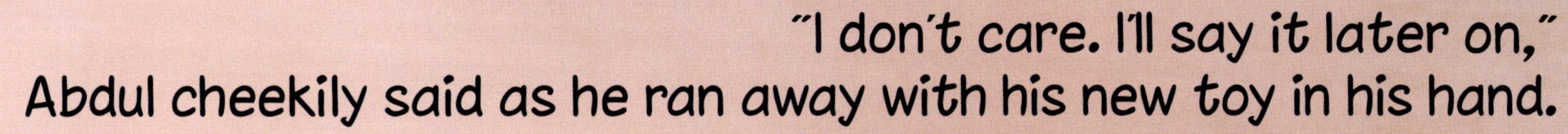

"I don't care. I'll say it later on,"
Abdul cheekily said as he ran away with his new toy in his hand.

"Stop!" said Yasmeen angrily "I'm talking to you!"

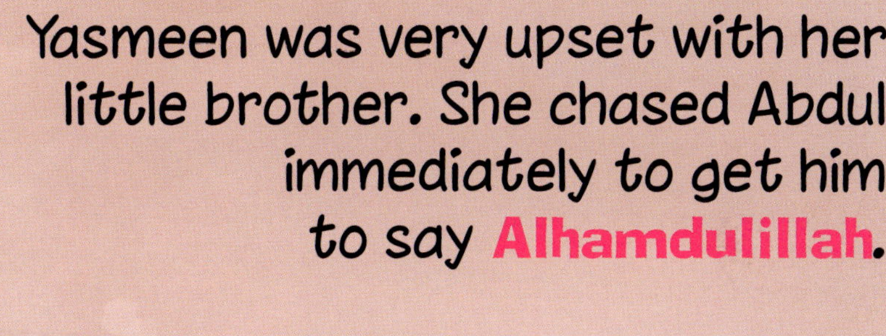

Yasmeen was very upset with her little brother. She chased Abdul immediately to get him to say **Alhamdulillah**.

"Catch me if you can?"
mocked Abdul.

As Abdul tried to run away from his sister,
he wasn't looking where he was going and tripped and fell over.

Abdul started to cry.

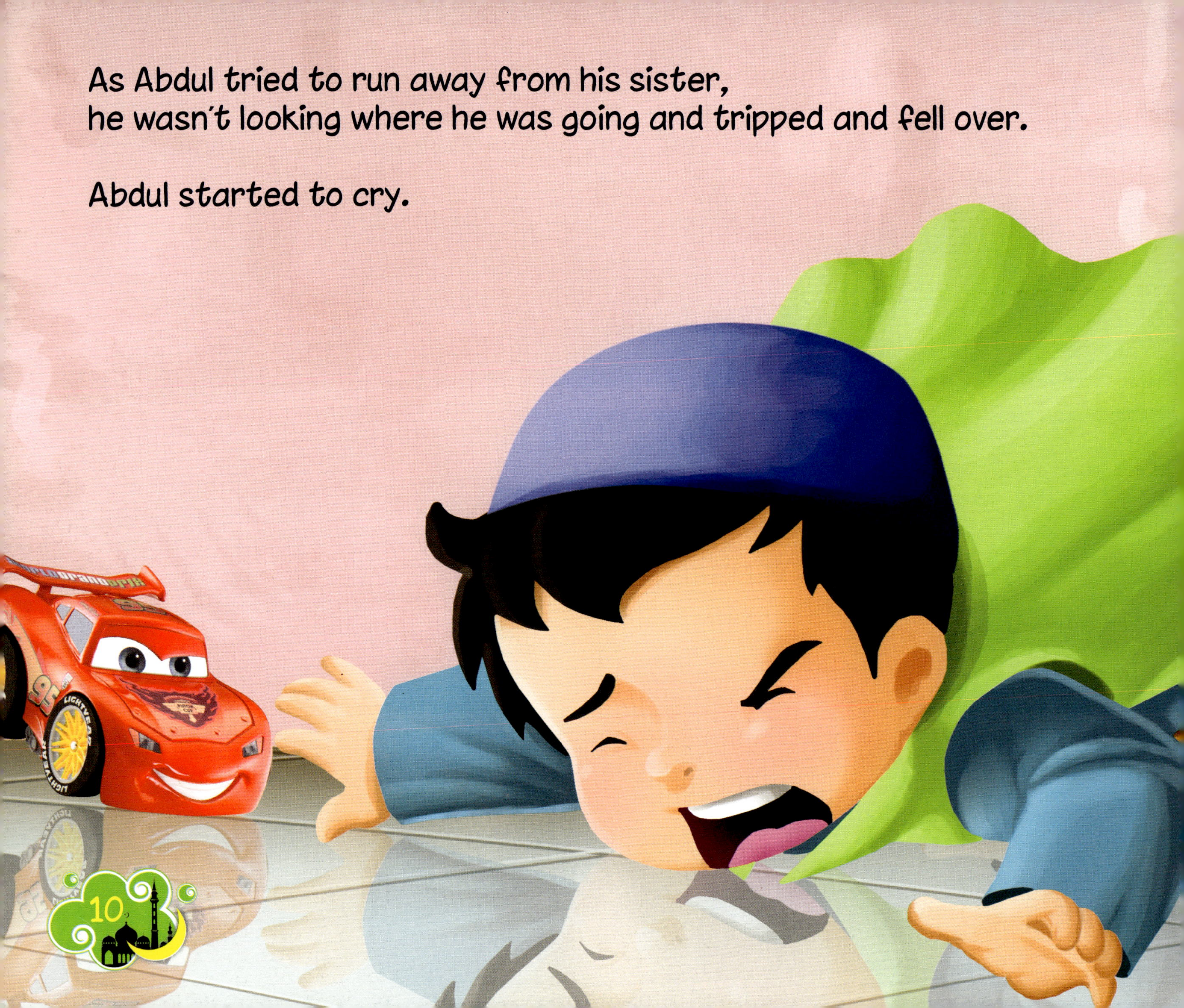

"Oh My Gosh," screamed Yasmeen, as she was immediately worried that her brother had hurt himself.

Yasmeen and Abdul's parents were in the next room and heard Abdul crying and immediately ran in.

"What happened Abdul? Why are you crying?" asked his concerned father.

"Sob, Sob... Yasmeen chased me and made me fall over," said Abdul trying to get his sister in trouble.

"Yasmeen, Why did you chase Abdul?" asked their mother, trying to find out what really happened.

"Abdul received a new toy car as a present and he didn't say **Alhamdulillah**.

My teacher said that we have to say **Alhamdulillah**, if we receive any blessing or bounty from Allah.

I only wanted Abdul to say, **Alhamdulillah**, as I know it's important to thank Allah when we receive any gift.

But, he refused to listen to me, so I chased him," Yasmeen tried to explain.

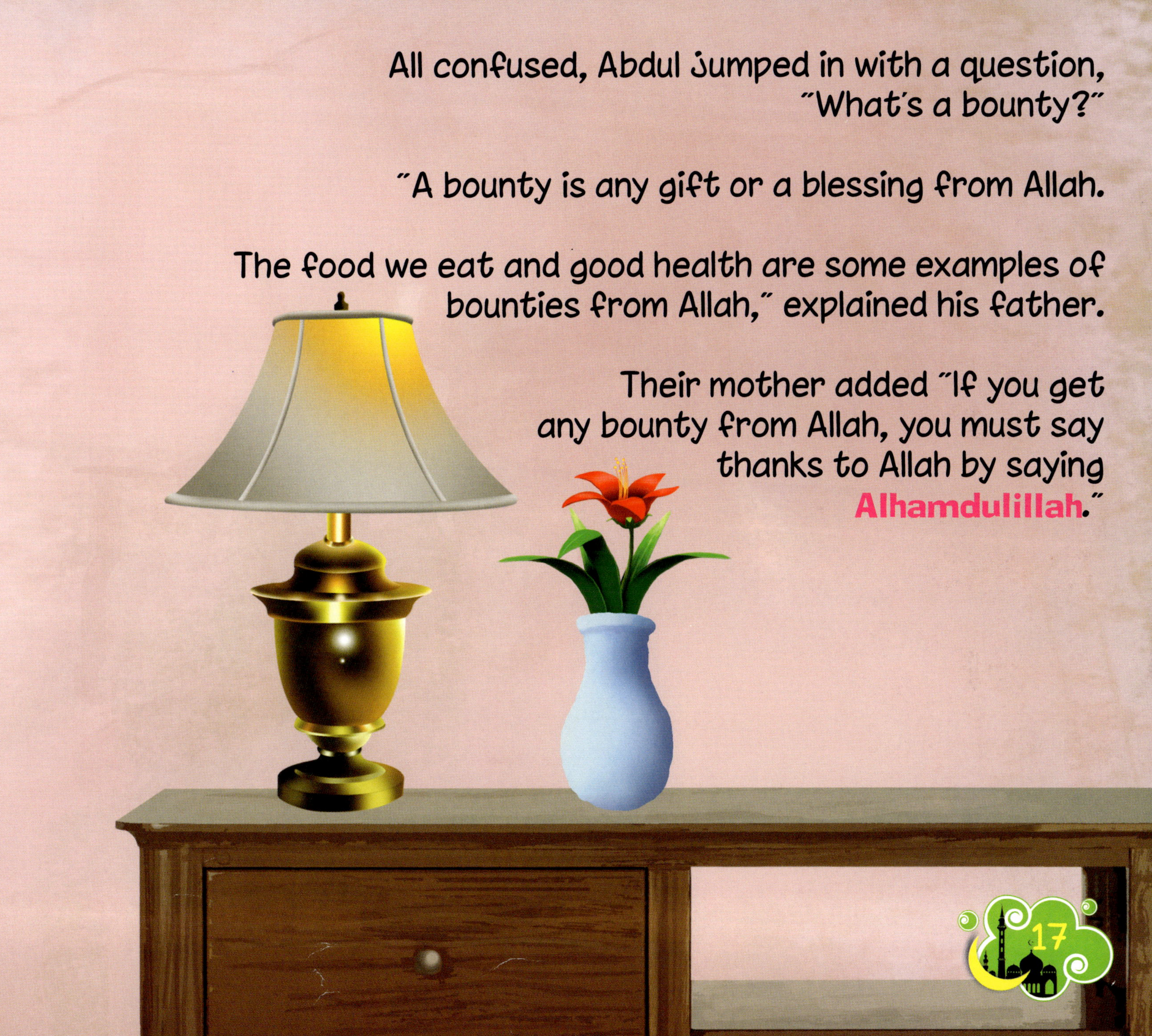

All confused, Abdul jumped in with a question, "What's a bounty?"

"A bounty is any gift or a blessing from Allah.

The food we eat and good health are some examples of bounties from Allah," explained his father.

Their mother added "If you get any bounty from Allah, you must say thanks to Allah by saying **Alhamdulillah**."

"Now I understand, so a gift like a toy car is also a bounty from Allah?" asked Abdul.

"Yes, correct Abdul," said his mother whilst nodding her head.

"Can I say **Alhamdulillah** now?"
asked Abdul, sadly.

"Of course you can, it's never too late to
thank Allah for what he has given us,"
said his mother now smiling.

Abdul was so happy now, he yelled at the top of his voice

"ALHAMDULILLAH,"

so the whole street could hear him.

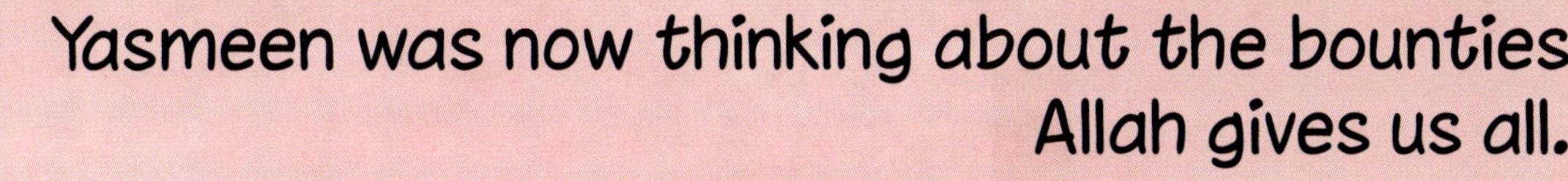

Yasmeen was now thinking about the bounties Allah gives us all.

"So, even though Abdul fell down, he didn't hurt himself, is this also a bounty from Allah?" asked Yasmeen.

"That's right, dear. When Allah protects us from bad things, this is also a gift from Allah," explained their mother.

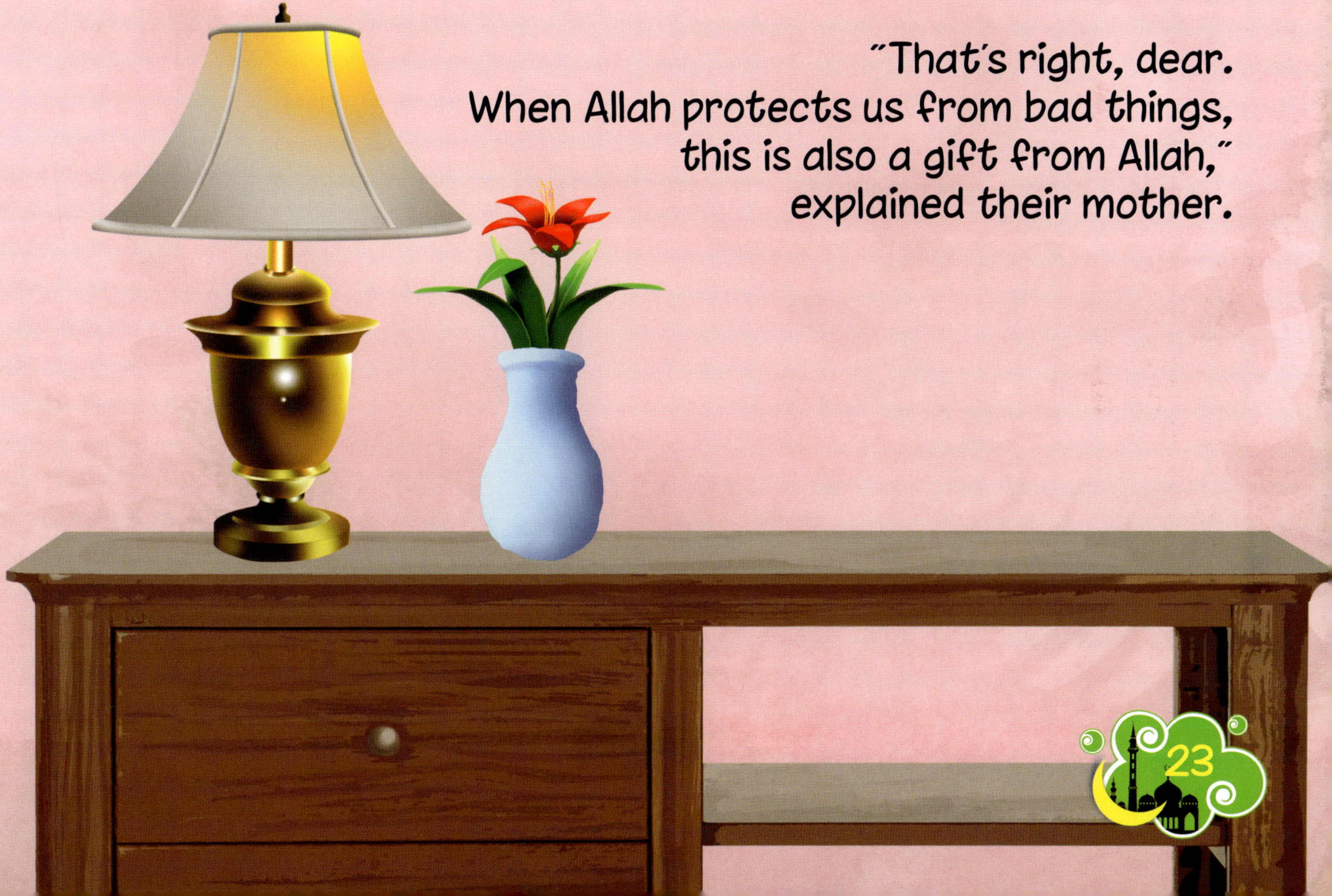

Their father reminded everyone "When we say **Alhamdulillah**, it helps us to remember Allah, and that Allah is in control of everything."

"From now on, if I get any gift or bounty from Allah I will definitely say **Alhamdulillah**," said Yasmeen happily.

"Me too," said an excited Abdul, who never wants to miss out on anything.